Introduction

Everyone is enthralled by snakes, from the smallest garden variety to the formidable rattlesnake. We at the Savannah River Ecology Laboratory (SREL) see this reaction almost every day of the year: thousands of people attend presentations given by us to learn more about this remarkable form of native wildlife. Whether we are talking to civic groups, schools, government organizations, or corporations, we meet people who are eager for knowledge about the natural history and ecology of snakes. It is through these encounters that we attempt to impart an enhanced appreciation for wildlife and the world in which we live.

Our intent in this brochure is to answer some of the most frequently asked questions about the snakes that occur in South Carolina and Georgia. We also provide information about the biology of these reptiles, as well as information and photographs useful for identifying the snake species of the region.

Coral snake

animals. For some readers this brochure should help replace fear of snakes with respect for them. For everyone we hope to enhance their experience in future encounters with the snakes of the region.

SREL is a research laboratory of the University of Georgia located on the U.S. Department of Energy's Savannah River Site (SRS) in South Carolina, bordering the state of Georgia. Here our research has uncovered a wealth of ecological knowledge of snakes native to the two-state region. In fact, more is known about the ecology of snakes on the SRS than in most regions of North America or the world.

Black rat snake

Authors of this brochure are actively engaged in field research and have participated in educating the general public about snakes. Our objective is to communicate our own knowledge about and experiences with this fascinating but greatly maligned group of

Corn snake

1

About Snakes

Snakes are reptiles characterized by elongated bodies and a lack of limbs. Distributed through most parts of the world, they range in length from 5 inches to more than 30 feet. They are closely related to lizards, but do not have external ears or eyelids.

The skin of a snake is dry and scaly, not slimy like some people believe. Snake scales are made of keratin, the same substance that makes up your fingernails.

Rough green snake searching for prey

A snake has a forked tongue that is used to "sample" microscopic particles from the air that are then put into a special organ in the roof of the mouth. This structure, called the Jacobson's organ, is highly sensitive to chemicals, like the nose of a blood hound. But rather than smelling, as we do, snakes "taste" the air. A snake flicking its tongue at you is merely trying to figure out what you are.

Racer tongue

Breeding occurs during spring or fall. Some species lay eggs in early summer; embryonic snakes develop in about two months and hatch in late summer or early fall. Snakes that give birth to live young also tend to have their young in late summer.

Outside temperatures affect the activity of snakes. Because they cannot generate their own body heat like mammals and birds can, snakes remain relatively inactive when it is too cold. They also cannot tolerate extremely high temperatures; therefore, most snakes are active during mild temperatures. During the spring and fall, most snakes tend to be active in the daytime; during the summer, activity may be restricted to warm nights, especially after a rain.

All snakes eat animals, not plants. The primary food items of most snakes are insects, fish, amphibians, birds, rodents, eggs, and other reptiles. Some species are selective feeders, whereas others eat a broad range of food items.

The most common form of defense by snakes, like other reptiles, is avoidance. At the first sign of danger, they usually flee. Any other defensive behavior by a snake, such as biting, striking, and so on, is usually a last resort.

Snakes are a natural and exciting component of the environment, as they have been for the past 160 million years. Their many unusual characteristics have long fascinated humans.

Hatching eastern hognose snake

Glass lizard

Four species of glass lizards, which look like snakes because they have no legs, occur in Georgia and South Carolina. Unlike snakes, glass lizards have eyelids and ear openings. Most glass lizards are found in pinewoods habitats with sandy soil. All are harmless.

Biodiversity

South Carolina and Georgia are fortunate to have among the the highest biodiversity of snakes in the United States. South Carolina has 38 species of snakes and Georgia has 40. Two species (the eastern indigo snake and the striped crayfish snake) are found in Georgia, but not South Carolina.

Snakes in South Carolina and Georgia range in size from the diminutive earth snake, which rarely exceeds 12 inches in length, to the eastern indigo snake, which may grow to more than 8 feet long. Although most species of snakes found in the Southeast are non-venomous, and thus harmless to humans, six venomous species do occur in the region. Five of these are pit vipers (family Viperidae) and include the cottonmouth, copperhead, pigmy rattlesnake, canebrake (or timber) rattlesnake, and the largest  rattlesnake in the world, the eastern diamondback. The other venomous species is the secretive, seldom-seen coral snake, a member of the cobra family (family Elapidae).

Ringneck snake

Ribbon snake in a wetland

evident in the coastal plain regions of South Carolina and Georgia.

The rich diversity of snake species in South Carolina and Georgia makes this region ideal for observing and learning about the snakes that share the area with us.

Glossy crayfish snake in a swamp

The high diversity of snakes in South Carolina and Georgia is due primarily to the warm, moist climate and the wide variety of habitats found in the southeastern United States. Snakes can be found from the mountains of northern Georgia to the barrier islands along the Atlantic coast. Some snakes are restricted to very specific habitats, such as the southern hognose snake, which in South Carolina and Georgia is found only in the sandhills communities of the Coastal Plain. Others, such as the black racer, can be found in almost any habitat. Aquatic habitats frequently support a high diversity of snake species, as is

Hardwood habitat

Snakes in Your Backyard

It is no surprise that snakes can be found in most backyards, parks, and woodlands in urban parts of South Carolina and Georgia. A variety of small and a few large species occur in the cities and towns of the

Earth snake

two-state region. Many species are secretive, spending most of their time underground or under cover. Active gardeners may occasionally see small ringneck, worm, red-bellied, brown, earth, and crowned snakes. None of these species are much bigger than a large earthworm and they do not bite. These species are often discovered under pieces of lumber, shingles, metal, or other yard debris.

Several larger snake species also frequent backyards, especially corn and rat snakes, as well as racers. All will eat mice, rats, and occasionally birds and their eggs. Snakes often take refuge in piles of brush or firewood. Chicken coops and barns sometimes harbor snakes searching for rodents or eggs. Water snakes, especially banded water snakes, are occasionally found

Common garter snake by a backyard pond

in neighborhoods that border streams, swamps, or farm ponds. In most cases, if cover and prey items are absent from a yard, then any snakes encountered are probably moving through the area. If a nearby woodlot is replaced with a new housing development, displaced snakes may be looking for a new place to live.

Snakes are fascinating animals and many are strikingly beautiful. As more and more people crowd into areas where snakes live, encounters between humans and snakes will increase. Be assured, however, that if your backyard contains snakes, it is probably a healthy place for you to live as well.

Searching for snakes under debris

Conservation

Snakes are important components of ecosystems because they play major roles as both predators and prey. Some snakes are specialized in their food preferences, such as the rainbow snake, which feeds primarily on American eels. Other snakes will eat almost anything. For example, the cottonmouth will eat fish, frogs, other snakes, rodents, birds, and carrion. Snakes are important foods for hawks and great blue herons, among other animals.

Scarlet snake

Pine snake in sandhills

in a river or stream, but also to assess how much might be moving into terrestrial food webs or to other aquatic systems.

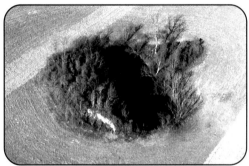
Agricultural clearing around a Carolina bay wetland

Many snakes are important economically because they eat rats, mice, and other animals deemed to be pest or nuisance species. Adult rat snakes in captivity can eat 2-3 rats every two weeks—52-78 rats per year for one snake! Wild snakes may not find this many rats in a year, but clearly one snake could have a significant positive economic impact by reducing the potential for some serious diseases (e.g., hanta virus, Lyme disease) that are enhanced by high rodent populations.

Top-level predators like snakes can accumulate toxins and transport them from one area to another. For example, mercury is found to some extent in many waters in Georgia and South Carolina. Water snakes have been used not only to detect the presence of mercury

Like many species, snakes are declining in numbers as a result of human activities. The threats to snakes and other wildlife are many, but primarily stem from lost and altered habitat. If large areas of specific habitats are reduced by agriculture, pine plantations, or commercial development, then species requiring more natural habitats may disappear or may persist only in very reduced areas. The direct and indirect effects of human activities not only affect snakes, but entire communities of animals and plants.

Typical sandhills habitat

Habitat loss due to development

Snakes as Pets

Snakes can be fairly easy to keep as pets and are very popular with some pet lovers for just that reason. Most snakes are very low maintenance. Some eat fairly infrequently, living on the occasional mouse or frog. Also, because they do not eat often, they produce very little waste.

Snakes take up little space. An aquarium with a well-sealed screen top or similar-sized wooden cage makes an ideal enclosure for many snakes and can be kept almost anywhere.

Typical home snake cage

Another advantage of snakes as pets is that they are quiet, which is important to some people—and especially to their neighbors. Also, a healthy snake can be an attractive and interesting pet for many years.

Thus, keeping a pet snake requires only a suitable container, a source of heat, a hiding spot, and food and water.

Included among the easy-to-keep species native to this area are corn snakes, rat snakes, and kingsnakes. All adapt well in captivity and can be fed live or frozen mice available at local pet stores. Keep in mind, however, that in the state of Georgia it is illegal to keep a native snake without special permits. And, of course, no one should ever keep a venomous snake as a pet.

If you are interested in befriending a snake, many books are available that can help you choose the most appropriate pet snake. With some time and effort, you can keep a pet snake and learn more about the habits of these intriguing animals.

Georgia

Of the 40 species of snakes that occur in the state of Georgia, only one is considered legally threatened—the eastern indigo snake. This species is recognized at the federal and state levels and, therefore, is protected from any form of direct take, including killing, harassing, collecting, or indirect take, such as habitat destruction.

Although no protection is afforded venomous snakes in Georgia, all non-venomous species are protected under the state's nongame species law, which was enacted in 1977. This law states that it is illegal to have any nongame species not listed as an exception for any reason, even as a pet. However, the law excludes venomous species of snakes from this protection.

Of course, snakes can be obtained in Georgia for scientific or educational purposes if a permit is obtained from the Department of Natural Resources (DNR). Thus, a school or other educational institution may request a permit to keep an indigenous snake in order to learn more about its habits and behavior.

These laws are currently under review by the Georgia DNR and are subject to change in the future.

Eastern kingsnakes are usually even-tempere

the Law

South Carolina

South Carolina has no state laws governing the importation and possession of venomous reptiles, or the sale of native reptiles.

The only snake species currently protected under state law in South Carolina is the eastern indigo snake. The eastern indigo snake is a federally threatened species known to occur in Georgia, but whether it now occurs (or has ever occurred) in South Carolina is questionable. South Carolina lists 9 species of snakes in a category called "Species of Special Concern," which indicates that too little is known about the ecology of the species to know whether it should be protected.

A collecting permit is required in South Carolina for the collection of snakes that are used for scientific purposes or for propagation. The annual fee for the collecting permit is $10.00 and before renewal the permittee must provide a list of species collected and their disposition. The Wildlife Diversity Section of South Carolina's Department of Natural Resources (SCDNR) administers the Collecting Permit program.

These laws are currently under review by SCDNR and are subject to change in the future.

The southern hognose snake is a species of special concern

Frequently Asked Questions About Snakes...

How do you tell the difference between a venomous ("poisonous") snake and a non-venomous one?

This question has no easy answer and any snake that cannot be positively identified as harmless should not be picked up. Pit vipers have large, triangular-shaped heads, but so do non-venomous water snakes. Pit vipers have elliptical pupils, whereas all harmless snakes in the eastern United States have round pupils; but so do poisonous coral snakes. No single rule separates all of the venomous species from all of the harmless ones, except the presence of fangs.

Do harmless snakes ever interbreed with dangerous ones?

Although there are rare examples of similar species hybridizing in the wild, no instances are known of pit vipers or coral snakes breeding with non-venomous species.

Can the bite from a non-venomous snake such as a kingsnake or racer make a person sick?

The bite from these snakes is for the most part harmless. In fact, with routine cleansing with soap and water, even the chance of infection is very unlikely.

What can I put around my yard to repel snakes?

No surefire product will repel snakes from a yard, although some commercial products containing sulfur or naphthalene (mothballs) are sold with claims of doing so. The amount required to be effective against snakes would make the place unlivable for most everything else, including people.

Can a cottonmouth (water moccasin) bite under water?

Yes. Cottonmouths feed on water snakes and fish, which they often catch in water.

Probability of Snakebite

Venomous snakes of Georgia and South Carolina pose little threat to humans who learn to observe them but otherwise leave them alone. Lightning kills many more people every year than snakes do, and the probability of dying in a car accident far exceeds the chance of even being bitten by a venomous snake. By one account, several thousand people are bitten by venomous snakes each year in the United States, but fewer than 10 of these bites actually result in deaths. Also, as many as half of all bites by venomous snakes are mild or "dry" bites in which little or no venom is injected.

Snakes do not hunt humans; we are not their natural prey and are far too large for any U.S. species to eat. Thus, they have no reason to bite us unless provoked. Snakebites occur when a snake is frightened and we force it to react in self-defense instead of allowing it to escape.

Cottonmouth fangs

More than half of U.S. snakebite victims were bitten while handling the snake, and more than two-thirds saw the snake before being bitten, but attempted to kill, capture, or harass it. Or they failed to move away or maintain a safe distance. In most of these situations, snakebite would have been easily prevented by exercising good judgment.

Copperhead

Certain activities can increase one's chance of getting bitten by a venomous snake. Logs, vegetation, rocks, and other materials provide shelter to snakes and the food they eat. Be cautious when moving such materials and avoid placing your hands or feet where a snake could be hiding. Proper footwear, such as leather boots, can provide protection from snakebites by preventing the fangs of a snake from coming into contact with your feet or legs.

Never pick up a snake unless you are absolutely certain it is non-venomous. Young snakes are sometimes difficult to identify and their small size can give the false impression that they are harmless. Furthermore, occasional snakebites have resulted from snakes presumed to be dead. An injured, but still-alive snake, may strike unexpectedly.

By following these common sense rules, you can enjoy the outdoors without becoming a snakebite victim.

Two young cottonmouths exhibiting color variation that is not uncommon in native snake species.

In Case of Snakebite...

Snakebites from native species are a rarity in both South Carolina and Georgia. However, a few bites still occur every year. The proper response to a venomous snakebite involves both what to do and what not to do. Before snakebite treatment is necessary, the snake must be venomous. You can become familiar with the snakes of the region by studying the pictures and descriptions in this brochure. If you can be sure that a non-venomous (harmless) snake did the biting, you have little to worry about. Washing the scratched area with soap and water is usually sufficient. However, a venomous snakebite can be very serious. The following is a list of what to do and not to do if bitten by a venomous snake:

Canebrake rattlesnake

The DON'Ts

- Do not eat or drink anything, including alcoholic beverages or medicine.
- Do not run or engage in strenuous physical activity.
- Do not cut into or incise bite marks with a blade.
- Do not apply a constrictive tourniquet.
- Do not use a stun gun or other electrical shock.
- Do not freeze or apply extreme cold to the area of the bite.

The DOs

- Try to stay calm!
- Keep the bitten body part below heart level and remove rings, watches, and tight clothing.
- Try to identify the offending snake if you can do so easily without putting yourself at risk or wasting valuable time.
- Get to the nearest hospital or emergency medical facility immediately.

Pigmy rattlesnake

The universally accepted treatment for serious snakebite is the use of antivenin or snakebite serum, which should only be administered by a medical doctor. If local doctors are unsure of the correct antivenin to use, advise them to contact the American Association of Poison Control Centers (1-800-222-1222).

Medical doctors who have experience with bites of venomous snakes of the United States do not completely agree on the details of first-aid treatment for snakebites. However, most doctors believe that the DOs and DON'Ts listed here have the highest probability of success in most situations involving venomous snakebites.

The best advice is to learn all of the snakes found in your region and avoid the venomous ones. If you are bitten by a venomous snake, remember to stay calm and get to the nearest hospital quickly.

Field herpetologists consider car keys (and a car) to be the best snakebite kit.

Quick Guide to Snakes

	Size	Identifying features	Identifying features	Size	
Banded water	Medium 2-3.5 ft.	Dark bands across back. Red bands on sides. (*page 15*)	Dark gray, dark blotches on sides and top. Often with stripe down center of back. Very small rattles. (*page 26*)	Small 1-2 ft.	**Pigmy rattler** DANGER
Northern water	Medium 2-3.5 ft.	Dark crossbands toward head, blotches toward tail. Half-moons on belly. (*page 15*)	Rattles. Dark V-shaped crossbands. Often with rust-colored stripe down back. (*page 26*)	Large 3-5 ft.	**Canebrake rattler** DANGER
Corn	Large 2-5 ft.	Red-orange blotches outlined in black. Belly white and black checkered. (*page 22*)	Rattles. Huge, thick body. Dark diamonds outlined by light scales. (*page 26*)	Very large 3-6.5 ft.	**E. diamondback rattler** DANGER
Mole	Medium 2.5-4 ft.	Uniform brown or with reddish brown spots. (*page 23*)	Dark bands across back, red bands on sides. (*page 15*)	Medium 2-3.5 ft.	**Banded water**
Copperhead	Medium 2-3 ft. DANGER	Dark brown bands "hourglass" shaped (wide on side and narrow in middle). (*page 25*)	Wide dark bands. Tail usually black. White upper lip. (*page 27*)	Large 2-4.5 ft. DANGER	**Cottonmouth**
Eastern hognose	Medium 2-3 ft.	Upturned pig-like nose. Spot color variable. Underside of tail lighter than belly. (*page 19*)	Black markings but no distinctive pattern. Belly plain whitish. (*page 14*)	Large 3-5 ft.	**Green water**
Southern hognose	Small 1-2 ft.	Upturned snout. Distinct dark blotches. Underside of tail same color as belly. (*page 19*)	Very dark body. Bands may be difficult to see. White upper lip. (*page 27*)	Large 2-4.5 ft. DANGER	**Cottonmouth**
Pigmy rattler	Small 1-2 ft. DANGER	Light gray, dark blotches on sides and top. Often with stripe down center of back. Very small rattles. (*page 26*)	Dark brown blotches down middle and sides of back. Thick-bodied. (*page 14*)	Large 3-5 ft.	**Brown water**

Quick Guide to Snakes

	Size	Identifying features	Identifying features	Size	
E. kingsnake	Large 3-5 ft.	Black body with "chain" of white or yellow rings. *(page 23)*	Body shiny bluish black. Chin may be reddish. *(page 25)*	Very large 4-8 ft.	**Indigo**
Rainbow	Medium 2.5-4.5 ft.	Glossy with red and black stripes. May have yellow chin. Black spots on belly. *(page 21)*	Black body, with some white areas between scales. Chin light. *(page 22)*	Very large 3.5-7 ft.	**Black rat**
Mud	Large 3-5.5 ft.	Shiny black back, red or pink triangles on sides. Harmless spine on tip of tail. *(page 20)*	Long and slender. Black also on belly, often with white chin. *(page 21)*	Large 3-5 ft.	**Racer**
Black swamp	Small 0.5-1.5 ft.	Shiny black back. Reddish belly. In aquatic habitats. *(page 16)*	Dark blotches on gray body. Stripes near head. *(page 22)*	Very large 4-6.5 ft.	**Gray rat**
Red-bellied water	Medium 2.5-4 ft.	Belly red or orange-red. Back usually plain brown. *(page 14)*	Slender body. Black head grading to brown on body. *(page 21)*	Very large 4-7 ft.	**Coachwhip**
Green water	Large 3-5 ft.	No distinctive pattern. Belly plain whitish. *(page 14)*	Rattles. Dark V-shaped crossbands. May be almost black. *(page 26)* DANGER	Large 3-5 ft.	**Timber rattler**
			Dark blotches on yellowish tan or gray body. Belly solid white. May hiss loudly. *(page 23)*	Large 4-6 ft.	**Pine**
Eastern hognose	Medium 2-3 ft.	Upturned pig-like nose. Melanistic (black) color phase dark to solid black. *(page 19)*	Dark blotches on pale brown or yellow body. Stripes near head. Belly dusky, blotched. *(page 22)*	Very large 4-6.5 ft.	**Gray rat**

Quick Guide to Snakes

	Size	Identifying features	Identifying features	Size	
Green	Medium 1.5-3 ft.	Light green back, with white or pale yellow belly. May be bluish when dead. (*page 22*)	Black or slate gray back. Yellow or golden collar. Yellow belly, often with large black half-moon spots. (*page 19*)	Small 0.5-1.5 ft.	**Ringneck**
Garter	Medium 1.5-3 ft.	Usually green or olive back with three yellowish stripes down body. Relatively stout-bodied, about as thick as your thumb. (*page 18*)	Belly plain red or orange. Three spots on neck. Back may be gray, black, or brown. (*page 17*)	Small 0.5-1 ft.	**Red-bellied (dark phase)**
Ribbon	Medium 1.5-2.5 ft.	Slender greenish body. Three yellowish stripes down body. (*page 17*)	Glossy with red and black stripes. Black spots on belly. (*page 21*)	0.5-1 ft. at hatching	**Rainbow (juvenile)**
Queen	Small 1-2 ft.	Yellow stripe on lower sides of body. Four brown stripes on belly. (*page 15*)	Red triangles may connect across top. Harmless sharp tail spine. (*page 20*)	0.5-1 ft. at hatching	**Mud (juvenile)**
Striped crayfish	Small 1-2 ft.	Very shiny. Brown back with very broad yellow stripes on lower sides. Belly may have spots. (*page 16*)			
Black swamp	Small 1-1.5 ft.	Shiny black back. Belly bright red. (*page 16*)	Rings around body, including belly. Red rings next to black. Red nose. (*page 24*)	Small 1-2 ft.	**Scarlet king-snake**
Glossy crayfish	Small 1-2 ft.	Shiny back, brown or olive-brown. Two rows of black spots on belly. (*page 16*)	Rings around body, including belly. Red rings next to yellow rings. Black nose. (*page 27*) [DANGER]	Medium 1.5-3 ft.	**Coral**
Yellow rat	Very large 4-6.5 ft.	Yellow or greenish yellow back with four dark stripes down body. (*page 22*)	Belly white. Snout red. Red blotches next to black. (*page 24*)	Small 1-2 ft.	**Scarlet snake**

Quick Guide to Snakes

	Size	Identifying features	Identifying features	Size	
Cottonmouth (juvenile) — DANGER	0.5-1 ft. at birth	Wide reddish brown crossbands. Broad, dark stripe through eye. Tip of tail yellow. (*page 27*)	Dark brown square blotches down center of back and on sides. (*page 14*)	0.5-1 ft. at birth	**Brown water** (juvenile)
Red-bellied water (juvenile)	0.5-1 ft. at birth	Boldly patterned with dark blotches. Banded water snake babies are similar. (*page 14*)	Brown back with two rows of small black dots. (*page 17*)	Small 0.5-1.5 ft.	**Brown**
Juvenile copperheads — DANGER	0.5-1 ft. at birth	Hourglass bands like adults. Tail tip yellow. (*page 25*)	Plain brown back and pinkish belly. Pointed head. Spiny tail. (*page 20*)	Small 0.5-1 ft.	**Worm**
Racer (juvenile)	0.5-1 ft. at hatching	Row of dark brown or reddish blotches down center of back. Reddish eye. (*page 21*)	Black head with black "collar." Back is light brown, belly whitish. (*page 24*)	Small 0.5-1 ft.	**Southeastern crowned**
Coachwhip (juvenile)	1-1.5 ft. at hatching	Brown body with numerous crosslines the length of the body. (*page 21*)	Brown back with pale sides. Dark head. Dark line through eye. (*page 20*)	Small 0.5-1 ft.	**Pine woods**
Rat snake (juvenile)	0.5-1.5 ft. at hatching	Grayish body. Dark blotches down center of back and sides. (*page 22*)	Belly plain red or orange. Three spots on neck. Back may be gray, black, or brown. (*page 17*)	Small 0.5-1 ft.	**Red-bellied** (light phase)
Pigmy rattler (juvenile) — DANGER	0.5 ft. at birth	Pattern similar to adults. Tip of tail greenish yellow. (*page 26*)	Gray or brown back with no markings. Belly white or yellowish. Scales smooth. (*page 18*)	Small 0.5-1 ft.	**Smooth earth**
			Brown back and yellowish belly. Snout relatively pointed. Each scale with a line or keel. (*page 18*)	Small 0.5-1 ft.	**Rough earth**

FAMILY COLUBRIDAE: NON-VENOMOUS
generally harmless snakes such as kingsnakes, water snakes, and rat snakes

Eastern Green Water Snake—*Nerodia floridana*

Uncommon. This species is found most often in permanent isolated wetlands, in open areas with minimal tree cover. It is heavy-bodied and often more than 4 ft. long; the color of the back is nondescript gray or greenish-brown. The largest of the water snakes, this species has been known to reach lengths of more than 5 ft. Green water snakes feed on frogs, fish, and salamanders.

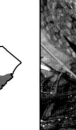

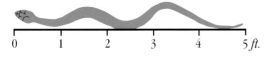

Female brown water snake with newborn babies

Brown Water Snake—*Nerodia taxispilota*

Locally abundant. This species is associated with stream, river, and swamp environments. It often attains a length of 4 ft. and is light brown on top with darker squares on the back and sides. The brown water snake is one of the most common snakes along rivers and streams within its geographic range and often is mistaken for the venomous cottonmouth. This snake frequently basks on tree limbs that overhang the water and it is not uncommon to see them at heights of 10 ft. or more. Brown water snakes feed almost exclusively on fish, especially catfish.

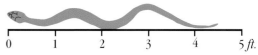

Red-Bellied/Yellow-Bellied Water Snake—
Nerodia erythrogaster

Locally common. This species is associated with aquatic environments of all types but occasionally is encountered several hundred feet away from permanent water. Its back is uniform dull black, dark gray, or brownish, and its belly is light red or orange, except those in west-central Georgia, which have light yellow bellies. Young individuals have a banding pattern similar to that of banded water snakes. Red-bellied and yellow-bellied water snakes feed on amphibians such as frogs, salamanders, and toads.

Juvenile red-bellied water snake

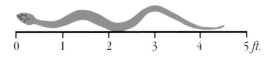

BANDED WATER SNAKE—*Nerodia fasciata*

Abundant. Being the most ubiquitous species of water snake, this species is found in all aquatic habitats, permanent or temporary. It enters brackish water and salt marshes. It is usually heavy-bodied and often more than 2 ft. long. Its color is variable but usually dark brown or reddish with crossbands. Like the northern water snake, the belly is marked with red blotches (see inset photo). Banded water snakes sometimes are mistaken for copperheads or young cottonmouths because of the banding pattern on the back. This water snake eats amphibians and fish.

Color variation is common in banded water snakes, as evidenced by the snakes pictured here.

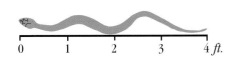

NORTHERN WATER SNAKE—*Nerodia sipedon*

Abundant. Found in most aquatic areas, this species usually is 2-3 ft. long but can attain lengths of 4 ft. Northern water snakes range in color from reddish brown to gray to brownish black, with dark crossbands on the neck and alternating dark blotches on the back and sides at mid-body. They eat small fish, salamanders, frogs, juvenile turtles, and crustaceans. The northern water snake has the largest geographic range of any water snake in the United States.

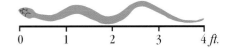

QUEEN SNAKE—*Regina septemvittata*

Locally common. This species is most frequently associated with running water habitats, particularly small streams. Queen snakes seldom reach a length of more than 2 ft. They are brown on top with an underside that is light yellow with 4 dark stripes. This species feeds on newly molted crayfish. Queen snakes do poorly in captivity, in part because of the difficulty of providing them with their specialized diet.

STRIPED CRAYFISH SNAKE—*Regina alleni*

Rare. This small species is found only in aquatic environments and generally inhabits aquatic vegetation in shallow water. Although difficult to find due to their secretive habits, in some locations this species has been found in higher numbers than any other snake species. The striped crayfish snake is dark brown on the back with three indistinct darker stripes running the length of the body; adults only grow to be about 20 in. long. Striped crayfish snakes feed almost exclusively on crayfish and both striped and glossy crayfish snakes have specialized teeth for holding onto hard-shelled crayfish.

Photo by Barry Mansell

GLOSSY CRAYFISH SNAKE—*Regina rigida*

Rare. This species is found in mucky areas along streams, in swamps, or along the edges of freshwater wetlands. Glossy crayfish snakes are shiny brown in color, with a double row of black spots down the belly. They seldom reach lengths of 2 ft. Their primary food is crayfish.

Herpetologists are uncertain whether this species truly is rare throughout its range or whether its habits are so poorly known that no one has found a good way to capture it.

BLACK SWAMP SNAKE—*Seminatrix pygaea*

Rare. This species is restricted to clean, heavily vegetated aquatic areas. Although known from only a few locations in Georgia and South Carolina, the black swamp snake can occur in enormous numbers at some sites. Adults are usually little more than 1 ft. long and are shiny black above with a bright red belly. Black swamp snakes feed on leeches, small salamanders, tadpoles, and fish.

Brown Snake—*Storeria dekayi*

Locally uncommon to common. This species is found in a diversity of habitats from moist to dry woodlands to swampy areas if abundant ground cover and litter are available. Frequently encountered in debris-covered sections of urbanized areas, this is one of the most common snakes in some residential areas of Georgia and South Carolina. Brown snakes are seldom more than 1 ft. long. Their general appearance varies from a soft brown or gray to dark brown; the belly is much lighter in color. Brown snakes feed on earthworms, slugs, and salamanders.

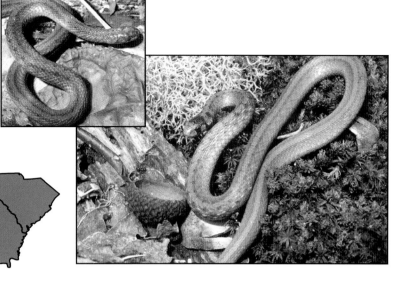

0   1 *ft.*

Red phase

Dark phase

Red-Bellied Snake—*Storeria occipitomaculata*

Locally common. Red-bellied snakes are primarily associated with moist woodland areas with abundant ground litter. They are slender and seldom reach a length of 1 ft. Their backs are usually reddish brown, but may be dark gray; the belly is some shade of red. Three light spots encircle the neck. This species feeds mainly on slugs and earthworms. Like brown snakes, red-bellied snakes may exhibit an unusual defense behavior when picked up--curling their upper lips upwards, making their mouths look larger.

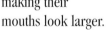

0   1 *ft.*

Eastern Ribbon Snake—*Thamnophis sauritus*

Uncommon to common. Ribbon snakes usually are found near aquatic areas, particularly along lake or swamp margins. They are more slender than the common garter snake (see next page), but otherwise are similar in general appearance. Ribbon snakes usually are less than 2 ft. in length, although occasional individuals may reach 3 ft. They feed on salamanders, frogs, and small fish and do well in captivity.

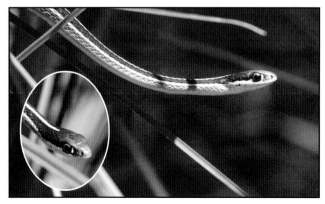

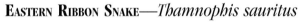
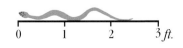

0   1   2   3 *ft.*

COMMON GARTER SNAKE—*Thamnophis sirtalis*

Uncommon to common. Common garter snakes are found in a diversity of habitats that are usually wet or damp, although not necessarily near permanently aquatic areas. They usually are less than 2 ft. long but occasionally reach lengths greater than 3 ft. Garter snakes are distinguished from all other South Carolina species except ribbon snakes by the presence of three yellow longitudinal stripes on a dark body. Garter snakes have black lines on their lip scales, whereas ribbon snakes do not. Although this pattern is common, some garter snakes in South Carolina and Georgia have a checkered body pattern with poorly defined stripes and a grayish body color. The belly of garter snakes is white or light yellow. This species gives birth to live young, sometimes having more than 50 babies. Garter snakes feed on frogs, toads, salamanders, fish, and tadpoles.

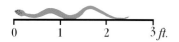

0   1   2   3 *ft.*

SMOOTH EARTH SNAKE—*Virginia valeriae*

Common. Smooth earth snakes usually are associated with deciduous woods or cut-over areas with abundant ground litter. They are extremely secretive. Seldom reaching lengths of 1 ft., these snakes are nondescript brown or gray on top with light bellies and smooth scales. This species feeds on earthworms and soft-bodied insects. Smooth earth snakes are inoffensive creatures that will not try to bite when picked up.

0   1 *ft.*

ROUGH EARTH SNAKE—*Virginia striatula*

Uncommon. Rough earth snakes are found in woodlands or areas having abundant ground litter and debris. They are similar in size and general appearance to the smooth earth snake mentioned above, but have rough (or keeled) scales. These are the smallest snakes native to Georgia and South Carolina. The rough earth snake feeds on earthworms and other invertebrates.

0   1 *ft.*

18

EASTERN HOGNOSE SNAKE—*Heterodon platyrhinos*

Common. Eastern hognose snakes characteristically are found in sandy habitats, including abandoned old fields and scrub oak forests. They often reach lengths of 2 ft. but seldom reach 3 ft. The color pattern of this species is highly variable. The best identifying feature of hognose snakes is the upturned snout. They feed on frogs and toads, but the young may eat crickets and other invertebrates. Specialized elongated teeth in the back of the jaw are used to "pop" toads and facilitate swallowing. Hognose snakes, especially the eastern hognose, are noted for their defensive displays of hissing, spreading their neck like a cobra, and even striking with their mouth closed. If pestered further, they will roll over on their back and play dead. Despite their bold act, they never intentionally bite humans (unless you smell of toads).

Melanistic (dark) color phase

Playing dead

Searching for toads

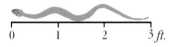
0   1   2   3 *ft.*

SOUTHERN HOGNOSE SNAKE—*Heterodon simus*

Rare. This species is found in habitats similar to those of the eastern hognose. Seldom more than 1.5 ft. long, southern hognose snakes are light brown with darker blotches. In contrast to the variability in color of the eastern hognose, the southern hognose always has the same color pattern. This species eats mostly toads, and occasionally frogs and lizards. Herpetologists fear for the future of this species because it has become very rare in some areas of its historical range.

0   1   2 *ft.*

RINGNECK SNAKE—*Diadophis punctatus*

Common. Ringneck snakes are restricted to moist, but not aquatic, environments. They are highly secretive and occur primarily in pine or deciduous woodlands with heavy ground litter. They may grow to lengths of slightly more than 1 ft. Ringneck snakes are black or slate gray on top with a yellow ring around the neck; the belly is yellow, orange, or red with a row of dark spots. This species feeds on earthworms, small snakes, lizards, salamanders, and frogs. Ringneck snakes rarely bite when picked up but will curl their tails to form a corkscrew that displays the brightly colored underside.

0   1 *ft.*

19

EASTERN WORM SNAKE—*Carphophis amoenus*

Common. Worm snakes, which are primarily restricted to woodlands, live underground in moist soil with decaying wood or heavy ground litter. Individuals seldom reach lengths of 1 ft. Their backs are brown or gray; their bellies pinkish. Worm snakes have hard, conical, sloping heads that help them burrow into soft soil and litter. They feed on earthworms and soft-bodied insects. Worm snakes never try to bite humans.

0   1 ft.

Photo by Barry Mansell

PINE WOODS SNAKE—*Rhadinaea flavilata*

Rare. This secretive species appears to be restricted to moist wooded areas, particularly in association with pine forests having abundant rotting logs and vegetation. Specimens are usually less than 1 ft. long. The body is brownish with a darker line passing through the eye; the belly is light in color. Pine woods snakes feed on small frogs, salamanders, and lizards. The isolated geographic distribution of this species in west-central South Carolina (see map below) is on the Savannah River Site, where about a dozen specimens have been found. Because of their rarity, herpetologists are uncertain whether they occur in other regions of southern South Carolina and Georgia and have simply not yet been discovered.

0   1 ft.

MUD SNAKE—*Farancia abacura*

Uncommon. Mud snakes primarily are associated with swamp systems and always are found in the vicinity of aquatic habitats. Individuals are heavy-bodied and often attain lengths greater than 4 ft. The back is shiny black or dark gray, and the belly is checkerboard red and black. Mud snakes feed mostly on large eel-like salamanders (amphiumas and sirens). This large, impressive snake will not bite a person when picked up, but will jab its tail against one's skin. The tail has a horny spine on its tip that is harmless to humans and presumably is used to prod its slippery salamander prey into swallowing position.

Juvenile mud snake

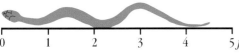

0   1   2   3   4   5 ft.

RAINBOW SNAKE—*Farancia erytrogramma*

Uncommon. Rainbow snakes are found in or around aquatic habitats, particularly cypress swamps. Individuals are heavy-bodied and frequently are more than 4 ft. long. This is the only snake in Georgia or South Carolina with a shiny black back with red stripes; the belly is yellow and red with rows of black spots. Rainbow snakes get their name from their beautiful red stripes, yellow chin, and the iridescent, bluish sheen of their scales in sunlight. Adult rainbow snakes feed primarily on American eels.

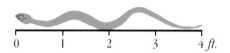
Juvenile rainbow snake

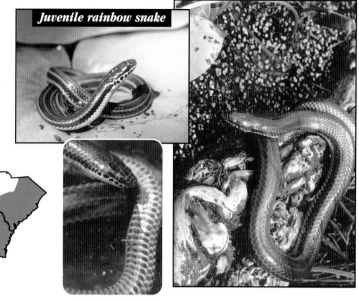

RACER—*Coluber constrictor*

Abundant. This species is found in a wide diversity of habitats and is particularly common in abandoned old fields, pine woods, and hardwood areas. Racers frequently are seen crossing highways during daylight hours. Adults are usually slender, 3 to 5 ft. long, and are black or dark gray all over except for a white chin. Racers feed on frogs, rodents, birds, lizards, and insects. Although the scientific name suggests that racers are constrictors, they are not. Racers eat their food while it is still alive, sometimes pinning the prey with their body before eating it.

Juvenile racer

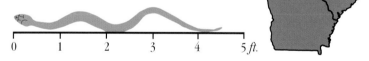

COACHWHIP—*Masticophis flagellum*

Uncommon. Coachwhips primarily are associated with dry, sandy habitats such as abandoned old fields, scrub oak forests, and sand dune areas. They also may occur in pine or hardwood habitats. Adults are slender, but frequently very long, often 5 to 7 ft. The unique adult color pattern grades from black on the head to a straw-colored tail. Young coachwhips are pale tan with light banding, but can be recognized by their large eyes, which are distinctive of this species. Coachwhips feed on lizards, snakes, small mammals, and birds.

Juvenile coachwhip

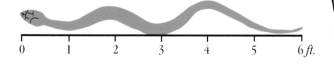

Rough Green Snake—*Opheodrys aestivus*

Uncommon. Green snakes are associated with thickly vegetated areas having vines, bushes, and shrubs, and are most commonly encountered along the edges of rivers and lakes. They often climb vegetation in search of prey, feeding on spiders, grasshoppers, and other invertebrates. Adults are very slender and seldom reach lengths of more than 2 ft. This is the only "green" snake in South Carolina and Georgia. The belly is light yellow. Green snakes are extremely well camouflaged and may be more abundant than people are aware.

0   1   2   3 ft.

Corn Snake—*Elaphe guttata*

Common. Corn snakes generally are associated with woodland habitats, including pine and hardwood areas. The usual adult length is 3 to 4 ft. The color pattern on the back consists of red or orange blotches; the "piano-keyboard" belly is light with black squares. Corn snakes feed on small mammals and birds. Like other rat snakes, corn snakes are constrictors that can easily subdue mice and small rats. They are excellent climbers and are able to crawl up walls or tree trunks.

0   1   2   3   4 ft.

Rat Snake—*Elaphe obsoleta*

Common. Rat snakes are found in a wide variety of habitats, but are most common in wooded or swampy areas. Adults frequently attain lengths of more than 4 ft. Coastal forms are olive with 4 dark stripes on the back; inland specimens range from black to light gray or brown with darker blotches and have a light belly with dark blotches. They feed on birds and their eggs as well as rodents, such as rats, mice, and squirrels. Known as the "chicken snake" in farming areas because they will readily eat chicks and chicken eggs, rat snakes also enter barns in search of mice and rats. Like corn snakes, they are very good climbers.

Black rat snake

Yellow rat snake

Juvenile rat snake

Gray rat snake

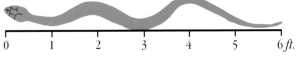

0   1   2   3   4   5   6 ft.

PINE SNAKE—*Pituophis melanoleucus*

Uncommon. Pine snakes are restricted to sandy habitats including abandoned old fields, scrub oak, or pine forests. Adults frequently reach lengths of 4 to 5 ft. The dorsal color is whitish or light gray with black blotches; the belly is plain white or gray. This species eats various rodents and may eat birds and lizards. Pine snakes are powerful constrictors, with adults being capable of capturing and killing rabbits and large rats. Defensive behavior includes opening the mouth, hissing loudly, and vibrating the tail.

Pine snake bluffing and hissing

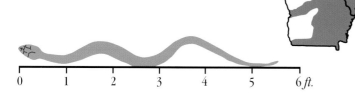

EASTERN/BLACK KINGSNAKE—*Lampropeltis getula*

Common. Kingsnakes occur in a wide variety of habitats. Although this species is considered terrestrial, it often is found in the vicinity of permanent or temporary aquatic areas. Adults often reach lengths of 3 to 4 ft. Eastern kingsnakes are black with light yellow or whitish crossbands whereas the black kingsnake, found in northwestern Georgia, is shiny black with scattered flecks of yellow. The belly is a combination of black and yellow. This kingsnake feeds on snakes (including venomous species), lizards, rodents, birds, and eggs-- even eggs scavenged from turtle nests. Experiments with kingsnakes have demonstrated that they are immune to the venom of rattlesnakes, cottonmouths, and copperheads.

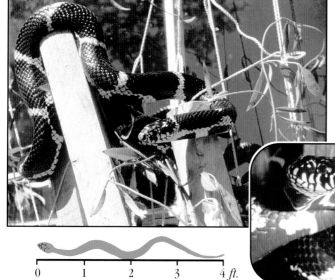

MOLE KINGSNAKE—*Lampropeltis calligaster*

Rare. This poorly known species presumably is restricted to areas of soft soil, including abandoned or cultivated fields. Adults reach 3 ft. and have light brown or pinkish backs with darker brown blotches. Mole kingsnakes are reported only from scattered localities within their geographic range. They are adept burrowers and are rarely encountered above ground except at night or after heavy rains. This species eats mainly rodents.

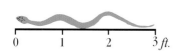

SCARLET KINGSNAKE/MILK SNAKE—*Lampropeltis triangulum*

Rare. This snake is restricted to wooded areas, primarily pine. Representing two subspecies, milk snakes are found in the mountains whereas scarlet kingsnakes are more coastal in distribution. Adult scarlet kingsnakes are usually less than 2 ft. long; milk snakes may reach lengths of 3 ft. The diet of these snakes includes baby rodents and small lizards and snakes. Red, yellow, and black rings completely encircle the body of scarlet kingsnakes, with red rings touching black rings. The pattern of milk snakes is less "ringed" and instead is characterized by saddle-shaped blotches. In scarlet kingsnakes the tip of the nose is usually red. The scarlet kingsnake is one of the most strikingly beautiful southern snakes and can easily be confused with the venomous coral snake, which is similar in appearance. Only someone who knows how to identify snakes should pick up any snake presumed to be a scarlet kingsnake.

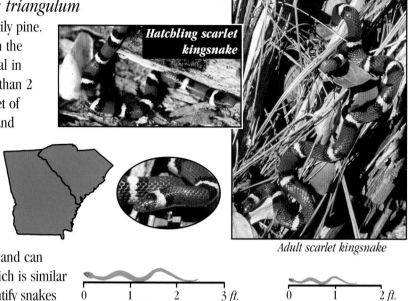

Hatchling scarlet kingsnake

Adult scarlet kingsnake

0   1   2   3 ft.
Milk snake

0   1   2 ft.
Scarlet kingsnake

SCARLET SNAKE—*Cemophora coccinea*

Uncommon. Scarlet snakes characteristically are associated with sandy soil habitats including pine woods, scrub oak forests, and abandoned old fields. Adults are slightly over 1 ft. long but seldom reach 2 ft. Typical individuals have red, yellow (or whitish), and black rings similar in size and position to those of scarlet kingsnakes but the rings do not encircle the body. This snake has a dull white belly and a pointed nose that is always red. It feeds mainly on reptile eggs but also will eat small lizards, snakes, and rodents. The scarlet snake is one of the most common snakes to fall into residential swimming pools in areas with sandy soil.

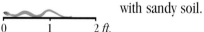
0   1   2 ft.

SOUTHEASTERN CROWNED SNAKE—*Tantilla coronata*

Uncommon. Southeastern crowned snakes are found in a variety of habitats but mostly in wooded areas with abundant ground litter and debris. This highly secretive snake seldom reaches 1 ft. in length. The back is light brown and the front portion of the head is black; there is a black band on the neck. The belly is light in color. Southeastern crowned snakes feed on centipedes, spiders, insects, and insect larvae. Although adept at capturing and eating venomous centipedes, crowned snakes do not bite when handled by humans.

0   1 ft.

Eastern Indigo Snake—*Drymarchon corais*

Rare. It would be difficult to confuse this huge blue-black snake with any other serpent in our area, except racers, which have white chins. The eastern indigo is the longest U.S. snake, reaching almost 9 ft. The young are about 1 ft. long and lighter than the adults, with a blotched pattern and brownish or reddish heads. The indigo snake has not been recorded in South Carolina but it does have a spotty distribution in Georgia. It lives in a variety of habitats but often is associated with gopher tortoise burrows in sandhills habitats. It is a true generalist, feeding on a variety of small animals including reptiles, amphibians, birds, and mammals. Indigo snakes readily eat venomous snakes such as rattlesnakes and cottonmouths and apparently are immune to the venoms of these snakes. Because it is a federally threatened species, it is illegal to collect or possess an indigo snake in captivity without proper permits.

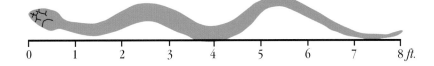

0   1   2   3   4   5   6   7   8 *ft.*

FAMILY VIPERIDAE: VENOMOUS

"pit vipers" whose fangs fold up against the roof of their mouth, such as rattlesnakes, copperheads, and cottonmouths

Copperhead—*Agkistrodon contortrix*

Uncommon to common. Copperheads are found in wet wooded areas, high areas in swamps, and mountainous habitats, although they may be encountered occasionally in most terrestrial habitats. Adults usually are 2 to 3 ft. long. Their general appearance is light brown or pinkish with darker, saddle-shaped crossbands. The head is solid brown. Their leaf-pattern camouflage permits copperheads to be sit-and-wait predators, concealed not only from their prey but also from their enemies. Copperheads feed on mice, small birds, lizards, snakes, amphibians, and insects, especially cicadas. Like young cottonmouths, baby copperheads have a bright yellow tail that is used to lure small prey animals.

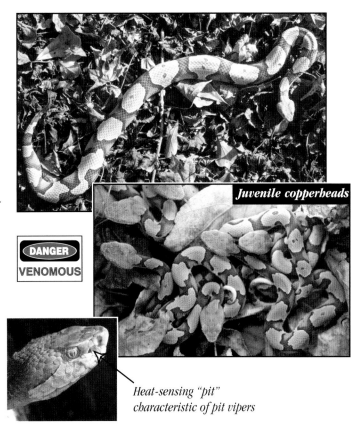

Juvenile copperheads

DANGER
VENOMOUS

Heat-sensing "pit" characteristic of pit vipers

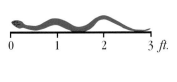

0   1   2   3 *ft.*

CANEBRAKE OR TIMBER RATTLESNAKE—*Crotalus horridus*

Common. This species occupies a wide diversity of terrestrial habitats, but is found most frequently in deciduous forests and high ground in swamps. Heavy-bodied adults are usually 3 to 4, and occasionally 5, ft. long. Their basic color is gray with black crossbands that usually are chevron-shaped. Timber rattlesnakes feed on various rodents, rabbits, and occasionally birds. These rattlesnakes are generally passive if not disturbed or pestered in some way. When a rattlesnake is encountered, the safest reaction is to back away--it will not try to attack you if you leave it alone.

Mountain form

Coastal plain form

DANGER VENOMOUS

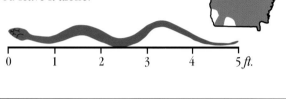

0 1 2 3 4 5 *ft.*

0 1 2 3 4 5 6 *ft.*

EASTERN DIAMONDBACK RATTLESNAKE— *Crotalus adamanteus*

Rare. This rattlesnake is found in both wet and dry terrestrial habitats including palmetto stands, pine woods, and swamp margins. Adults are frequently 3 to 5 ft. long and occasionally are more than 6 ft. Their basic color is light to dark brown with distinct diamonds of a combination of brown and yellow; the tip of the tail is solid black with rattles. Eastern diamondbacks feed on rabbits, rats, and squirrels. This snake, because of its huge size and potent venom, is considered by some to be the most dangerous snake in the United States.

DANGER VENOMOUS

PIGMY RATTLESNAKE—*Sistrurus miliarius*

Uncommon. Pigmy rattlesnakes may occur in association with wet areas in wooded habitats or swamps, scrub oak-longleaf pine forest habitats, or other wooded sites. Individuals are heavy-bodied, but usually are only slightly more than 1 ft. long. The general color of this snake is dull gray with dark gray or brown blotches on the back and sides. The small size of the pigmy's rattles make the "buzz" difficult to hear. This species is so small and well camouflaged that people seldom see pigmy rattlers that are coiled atop pine straw or dead leaves. This snake feeds on mice, lizards, snakes, and frogs.

Newborn pigmy rattlesnakes

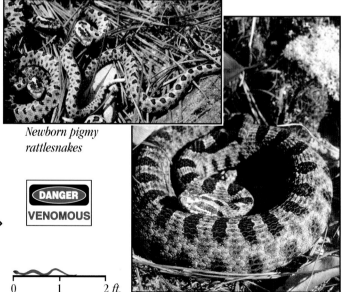

DANGER VENOMOUS

0 1 2 *ft.*

Cottonmouth (Water Moccasin)— *Agkistrodon piscivorus*

Dark phase

Abundant. Cottonmouths are found in association with every type of wetland habitat including estuaries, tidal creeks, and salt marshes; this species often wanders overland in search of food. Adults reach lengths of 3 to 4 ft. and often are heavy-bodied. The color pattern is variable, but the backs of adults are usually drab brown or olive with darker crossbands. The belly is a combination of dull 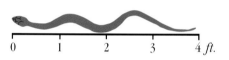 yellow and brown and the underside of the tail usually is black. This species is unquestionably the most common venomous snake found in wet- land habitat types. However, the harmless brown water snake, which is very common in aquatic areas frequented by humans, often is mistaken for the venomous cottonmouth. If disturbed, the cottonmouth will often stand its ground and give an open-mouthed threat display. Brown water snakes, when disturbed, will drop from overhanging tree limbs and flee.

Light phase

DANGER
VENOMOUS

0   1   2   3   4 ft.

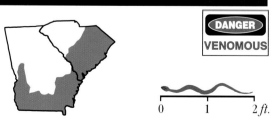

Juvenile cottonmouth

FAMILY ELAPIDAE: VENOMOUS
fixed-fang snakes such as cobras, kraits, and coral snakes

DANGER
VENOMOUS

0   1   2 ft.

Eastern Coral Snake—*Micrurus fulvius*

Rare. Eastern coral snakes are found in association with a wide variety of terrestrial habitats including wooded areas, fields, and margins of aquatic areas. Adults reach about 2 ft. in length. Red, yellow, and black rings encircle the body. The narrow yellow rings touch the red rings, a pattern distinguishing this species from the scarlet kingsnake and the scarlet snake. The nose is always black, followed by a wide yellow band. This snake feeds on small snakes and lizards. Coral snakes, which belong to the same family as Old World cobras and kraits, have short, fixed fangs in the front of the mouth. The potential seriousness of a bite from this species warrants a universal warning not to pick up a snake in this region of the country--no matter how pretty--without being certain of its identity.

Snakes in Southern Myths and Folklore

Perhaps no other animals have been the object of so much fear, misinformation, and misunderstanding as snakes. The following is a list of common southern myths regarding snakes and snake behavior and some possible explanations for these tales.

Snakes chase people.

FALSE! Many people who have spent time outdoors have a story about being chased by snakes. But  herpetologists, people who study reptiles and amphibians, never seem to have this experience—they find that snakes are always trying to escape. To understand this perceived behavior of a snake chasing someone, one must first realize that a snake has nothing to gain by chasing a person. A snake obviously could not eat a person and so is not looking for food. They are not vengeful and do not chase people out of sheer hate.

Rattlesnakes always add one rattle a year.

FALSE! A rattlesnake adds one rattle every time it sheds its skin. Snakes may shed several times in the  course of a year, each time adding a new rattle; rattles also may break off. Determining a snake's age by counting rattles usually results in an inaccurate estimate of the snake's age.

Snakes travel in pairs, the survivor seeking revenge if one is killed.

FALSE! Snakes do not travel in groups or pairs. They do not have any social bonds and would feel in no way vengeful if one of their number were to be killed. One possible explanation for this myth is that in a prime  habitat situation, multiple snakes of the same species could be encountered in a relatively small area. Another explanation could be related to typical reproductive behavior. During the mating season a male snake will trail a female snake much as a buck deer trails a doe during the rut. In either situation, one may make the incorrect assumption that the second snake seen was out for revenge.

A snake must coil before it can strike.

FALSE! Snakes can bite or strike from any position. Coiling does, however, increase the distance that a snake can strike.

Snakes go blind during the dog days of August.

FALSE! Snakes must shed their skins in order to grow. To help the old skin slide off, a gray-white lubricant is secreted under the old skin. This liquid is visible under the clear scale that protects the eye, making it look clouded over. This does, in fact, impair a snake's vision. Although snakes are not known to shed any more in August than in any other summer month, shedding blindness is the probable origin of this myth.